PiK & MiX

Butterflies & Poetry are Transcendent

First published & printed in 2004
Second Edition Published by 2Interact 2004
Printed in the UK by Deanprint Ltd

British Library Cataloguing in Publication Data available

ISBN: 0-9549192-0-3

Pik & Mix in aid of The RapeStoppers Campaign, care of Cosmopolitan Magazine UK.

A Loving Legacy

Compiled and Edited by Jeannette Slavinski
www.speechdramateacher.com
Layout, Artwork & Illustrations by Basia Ligman

Acknowledgements

The publishers and Jeannette Slavinski are extremely grateful for the booksellers of the UK who gave support for this project.

Grateful thanks to the Manchester Evening Newspaper, Stockport Express, Citizen, The Universe, Cosmopolitan Magazine, PURE radio for their media coverage and colleagues who gave their advice and support in the compilation of this book.

Special thanks to Basia Ligman on the book's 'Odyssean' journey, her loyal support and compelling artwork. Lord Eardley and Lady Barker who have written under pseudonyms.

We would like to thank all the poets for giving permission to permit their work to be published in this book.

Grateful acknowledgements are given, to the following organisations that believed in and supported Pik & Mix with sponsorship towards publication.

Ringway Airparks Ltd; The Belfry House Hotel; Gorvins Solicitors; The Lowry Hotel; Network X^n Ltd; Beluga Bar and Deanprint Ltd.

Special thanks to Jenny Hayes, (01625 501 765) - Agent to Jeannette Slavinski

For my Mum, her never ending encouragement
and
Daniel & Gabrielle

Contents   Page

Introduction

Hello and welcome to the 'Pik & Mix' Luminous Edition, independently aided in aid of The RapeStoppers Campaign.

Having read numerous accounts of rape victims' sufferings and meeting them first hand, I discovered many victims were too scared to speak out! Rape is forced violation of women's rights, a Criminal Offence. Thou shalt not rape. Rape happens anywhere, anytime, to anyone, by anyone regardless of the victim's age, creed or colour. Perpetrators use any means viable upon the innocent. How frightening is Date Rape, the new designer drug readily available? Rape is a Life sentence.

One young HIV orphan in South Africa who was repeatedly raped and then silenced for 'snitching' prompted me to become the 'silent voice' for victims torturous mental and physical ordeal.

Here in the UK we are fortunate that we can reach out and receive help, thanks to Cosmopolitan Magazine who are setting up a help line to help victims. Other Nations are not so fortunate.

Pik & Mix is a Benediction to all who have been raped or sexually assaulted.

So without further ado, I reached into my archives and donated my own lyricism and launched an appeal via the media for poets to send in their poetic license. To an overwhelming response, writing was selected from far and wide under four categories, spiritual, political, romantic and comedy, an abstract rendering, edition 1 sold out instantly. Bingo, the milk of human kindness creating further awareness and funding for the Rapeline Campaign.

The simple act of this goodwill enabling the success of the book includes you the buyer, to give the price of it to The RapeStoppers Campaign. The book itself is, in a sense, no more than a guarantee that your benevolence truly has gone where you aimed it - which, as all givers are aware, is a most satisfying thing to know.

To have a passion in your life is to live life to the full, to share one's passionate sweet success is nectar to the soul. Contained within the philosophy of this anthology are living words, independent insight, organic testaments to the will and temperament of the writers emotions, their passionate penmanship dedicated to a much needed cause, complimented by compelling photography, art work exclusive intimate views and interactive interviews.

Like a box of chocolates - Pik & Mix has something for every palette. Choose your favourite.

The net profits of Pik & Mix will be donated to The RapeStoppers Campaign.

Jeannette Slavinski

The RapeStoppers Campaign

The Rape Stoppers Campaign has been set up by Cosmopolitan Magazine UK. Cosmo are aiming to set up the first UK RapeStoppers help line. A 24-hour, 7 day a week phone line manned by trained counsellors, for women to call if they have been raped or sexually abused.

Cosmo are hoping to raise £500,000

Please send all enquiries to cosmo.mail@natmags.co.uk

Mr Blunkett's Ditty

Women of the UK United
Hail our voice outright
Support us in our campaign
Female's human rights.
Our sacred selves are
Precious to cherish
Honour, love
Alas, how many times
Are we abused
To Satisfy insatiable lust?
Without consent our
Resounding plea 'Stop'
Echoes far and wide,
Operative word being
'RAPE', painful fearful cry.
Many times we're silenced
Our tongues ripped out,
Beaten, drugged, imprisoned
Maimed and lewdly tortured.
Age, creed, colour has no
Barrier, to savage satyriasis
Victims traumatised within,
Life sentence of paralysis.

Hear our ditty Mr. Blunkett
House of Commons heed
Help us with our Rapeline
Freedom to call, 24/7 anytime

JS

To know the way and not practice is to be a soup ladle in the pot and not taste the flavour of the soup

BUDDHA

Show Me

Show me the stones which absorbed His blood
And the fragmented cross which He bore.
Show me the tomb where they laid Him to rest
And the scraps from the garments He wore.
Show me the tree where Judas hung
In shame for betraying a friend.
Show me Mary, His mother so pure
Who stayed with Him right to the end.
Show me the way to eternal life
Help me find the path which He trod.
Show me an image of His precious face.
Let me utter; 'My Lord and my God'.
Show me the room where he met with His men
After the dreadful deed had been done.
Show me O Lord your infinite love
I'm yearning to follow your son.

Barbara Eastham

Stoned

Music of Time

Once,
I was a violin,
Pert little corners, and curves
in all the right places.
Tone bright,
(sometimes strident in higher register),
agile with acrobatic arpeggios.

> Then,
> almost without noticing,
> I became a viola.
> Bigger, more fruity and rounded,
> with thoughtful reflective sound.

Now,
I fear I am becoming a cello.
Mellow, with huggable girth
and the resonance of years.

> Soon,
> I may even
> (perish the thought),
> become a double bass.

My consolation
in this accelerando passage
is to know that you will be there
caressing my strings
as you always have.

For only your bow
can make me sing.

Joyce Reed

Make the Bed

Make the bed before you get up, came the order from downstairs...
Half drowned by clinking tea cups and the clattering of chairs...
Make the bed before you get up!, now there's one to mull over.
I lay there wondering how to get myself from under the cover...
I slid to the left and then to the right, but the duck down duvet put up
A fight. The pillow joined in and tried to choke me, I gave up the
Struggle and lay quite still... until, the voice from downstairs
again...

Do you hear me,? Make the bed before you get up, breakfasts...
Nearly ready! I tried again but still in vain, my head was in a
daze...
Make the bed before you get up ... She's got some funny ways!
Snuggling back down to ponder the task, I'd tried my best to do as
She asked, make the bed before you get up, the things that woman
says!

JB

Toffee's

I`ll give thee wun, dun`t ask agin, ah canna think wot am doin..!
Must tha keep movin tha jaws in tempo wi me chewin.?
Nah look ere lad, I`ve arf a bag, there` plenty to go round...
it`s just that these are all 'little uns', a big un fer you I ain`t
found.

I`ll keep lookin fer wun, dunna fret, but like ah sed, I ain`t found wun
yet. Thee be patient, I`ll try another, cum nah lad must thee cry for tha
muther.? I`ll give thee wun, ah told thee afore, so pick tha chin up
off tha floor.

Art sure that these are the wuns yer fonder,? Not same as last lot..
makes me wunder.! Ah cud tell by the taste all lemony like, they'd
upset tha belly an make thee skrike.! I`ll give thee wun, this might
do
but to be on`t safe side.... I`ll give it a chew...

Yer doin it agin, yer startin to holler, nah look wot yerv dun, yerv
made me ...swoller.! Its tha own fault, there ain`t none left, ah wuz
thinkin of you, ah did me best. I tell thee wot, thee hold the bag...
ah think it`s only fair. An wen yer Mam buys you sum more.........
like a pal..... I`ll let thee share!

Ron Megan

Rape is taboo, a word which frightens people. On the streets of Manchester the interviewed public had their say.

Q. What do you think of Rape?

A. 'Women are too traumatised to give evidence in court, especially if its their husband. Male judges are not sympathetic to women's rape ordeals. Rape needs discussing in schools especially boys' schools.'

Anne King (Manchester)

An Obsession with Toilets

Mum's got an obsession with toilets
And she carries this notepad and pen
Then whenever she sees an unsuitable loo
She will give it a mark out of ten

She'll inspect all accessible toilets
At a restaurant, a pub or hotel
And whenever we're asked to a relatives house
She will go and inspect theirs as well

She doesn't like British facilities
and dislikes the French even more
Cos there's either a woman sat down with a box
Or a slot for some cash on the door

But my mum's got a trick to get round this
and whenever we're on holiday
she will always attempt to crawl under the door
Just so she won't have to pay

There is one good story I'll tell you
And believe me this story is true,
Just picture this scene at a service station
In the midst of a French public loo

My mum had just been to the toilet
and she picked up her bag off the floor
It was one of those loo's where you have to put cash
In a box that's attached to the door

But my mum's got this thing about saving
She's as charitable as she can be
So after she'd been she held open the door
And allowed this French lady in free

But there was something my mum failed to notice
If you do not put cash in the door
The door automatically locks from inside
And you can not get out anymore

Suddenly from inside the toilet
My mum heard a terrible shout
And the lady concerned started shouting in French
And she screamed at my mum 'let me out'

Others in the loo started staring
And because my mums French isn't good
She didn't understand what this lady had said
So she ran out as fast as she could

My mum sprinted straight down the car park
And dropped all her things on the floor
And never again has she entered a loo
Without putting cash in the door.

Hanna Sillitoe

ROOKIES. 19.35.
WOOLWHICH.

Thoughts on War

Millions of people that I never knew
I pay my respects too.
Their bodies lost little found
Lie buried in enemy or allied ground.

Husbands, fathers, brothers
Each day another thousand gone
Each bullet with a soldiers name on.

Crosses lie row in row
Gravestones fill the cemetarys
Poppies scatter the dead ground
As the hushed silence descends.

A unity brought from the dead
Those who fought for little,
But a hundred yards
A cross now rest at their head.

Rest in peace so many say,
'Sleep my friends,' I say
'Your duty is done be at ease
Soldiers be at ease.'

Kirsty Fawley

Q. What do you think about a Rape Help Line being set up 24/7 in this country?

A. 'I think it's very helpful, rape is a big issue in this country it is increasing every day, each month. It has a high rate in this country which affects the whole family the unity and the country itself. Rape is a main issue that people should be looking into.'

Salem Al Agel (Kuwait)

Angels, Angels, Angels all Around

Life

Life is such a precious gift
Live it while you may,
For the seconds just like raindrops
Fall and run away.
Fill it full of purpose
Every minute of the day,
For on the road of no return
We pass no more this way.
The thread of Life is fragile
When broken, cures are sought,
Though money can buy many things
Life cannot be bought.

Lillian Gertrude

Midwife's View

I first met Jenny when she was 36 weeks pregnant. A young teenage girl who was having her first baby. She was accompanied by her sister. This was, up until our meeting, a concealed pregnancy, only her sister knew. She found out only a week before they came to see me and had persuaded Jenny that she needed some antenatal care.

Jenny had been a victim of rape, and from the rape - a pregnancy. At 15, she had been abused by a family friend and this was her first time she had told anybody. She was crying, shaking, you could see the fear in her eyes as she spoke about her ordeal.

Over the following weeks, I spent a lot of time with Jenny and arranged to be there when she gave birth. The birth was something that Jenny feared the most. We agreed that no vaginal examinations would be performed to assess the progress of labour. The thought of them made her physically shake with fear. Thankfully, the labour progressed normally and quickly and Jenny gave birth to a baby boy who she named Ethan. At Jenny's request, she wanted Ethan to be adopted.

As a midwife looking after Jenny it was heartbreaking to watch. This young girl had her innocence taken away from her by somebody she trusted and at just 15 had given birth to a baby boy, who, at that point, she would never see again.

Fictitious names have been used in this testimony, to protect the innocent.

Louise Phillips

NO ONE
WILL EVER GET
MY VERSES
WHO INSIST UPON
VIEWING THEM AS
A LITERARY
PERFORMANCE

WALT WHITMAN

Talking Wire

Eve Bugs

A narrative for enacting

Allow me to introduce you to Eve Bugs.

Saw an ad in the newspaper, Hugh Hefner Seeks Bunnies.
Grooveeeeeeeeeeeeeeeeeeeeeeeeeeeeeeeeeeeeeeeeeeeeeeeeeeeeeeeeeeeeeeeeeeeeeeeeeeeeeeeee
My friend Penny bet me a guinea I wouldn't go to the audition. (Although
I didn't really know what a so called bunny was and being most impulsive
I decided to find out.) After all I was bored with my mundane job as a
confectioners assistant, like most women I craved sweet success and here
was my opportunity. So I covered myself in fake tan, bought a swimsuit
and a pair of stilettos.

There were hundreds of women at the roll call, some extremely glamorous
others merely wall flowers, but never-the-less waiting with bated breath!
Each one had been instructed to change into a breath taking corsage. 'Eve
Bugs.' Gosh that's me I thought as I hopped into a seductively lit room
almost tripping over my ankles, (well at least I had one foot in the door!!)
Mr. Diagio (the Chicago night club impresario,) was sat on a scarlet covered
chaise smoking a huge Cuban cigar. I had to walk up and down like a
mannequin and strike a pose, yet I'd never struck a pose in my life!
Marilyn Monroe immediately sprang to mind. 'Happy Birthday Mr.
President.)

Mr. Diagio said in this very American accent. 'Well Eve, why do you
wanne to be a Bunny Girl?' Which appeared to be the standard question. I
said, I love being admired in this wonderful bunny girl corset its so
flatteringly feminine. Well that was the icing on the cake, eye candy, he
hired me instantly. Bye Bye carrot cake, sugar daddy here I come.

All the bunnies had beautiful figures, think that's why we got picked.
Payment was a pound an hour, well paid but hard work. Eight hour shifts
in killer heels plus the Bunny Dip!!!

Schooling a bunny is not easy, flexibility of the spine is a must, carrying
a drinks tray aloft commands balance, ordering from the bar man needs

direction and the Bunny Dip, means bending over the table backwards without ones bosom falling out trying to smile without enacting a buck teeth effect!!!

Mother Bunny inspected before each shift making sure our nails were manicured, seams straight, bob tails perfectly fluffed, after all Bucks were in abundance tips and money talked. When sitting we had to keep our backs straight and cross our legs so they always looked long and lovely. I sat on Frank Sinatra's lap once for a photograph, while he rabbited on, 'Luck Be A Lady.' He couldn't wait to play pok-her (which refers to a rule in poker.) Old blue eyes loved to gamble.

There were always famous people in the casino but the ones who were the most generous were the Arabs, they were a novelty and extremely rich. If they took a shine to you dazzling jewellery, flowers and chocolates would arrive, they would wine and dine you in style, much to the dismay of the Maitre D.
Imagine me, Bunny Eve, fairy cake maker dining out in a second hand dress from a charity shop. Talk About School for Scandal.

It was a bizarre fantasy, a dream, a tease, so glam, so highly publicised, as if we were the most splendid creatures in the world.

JS

KN

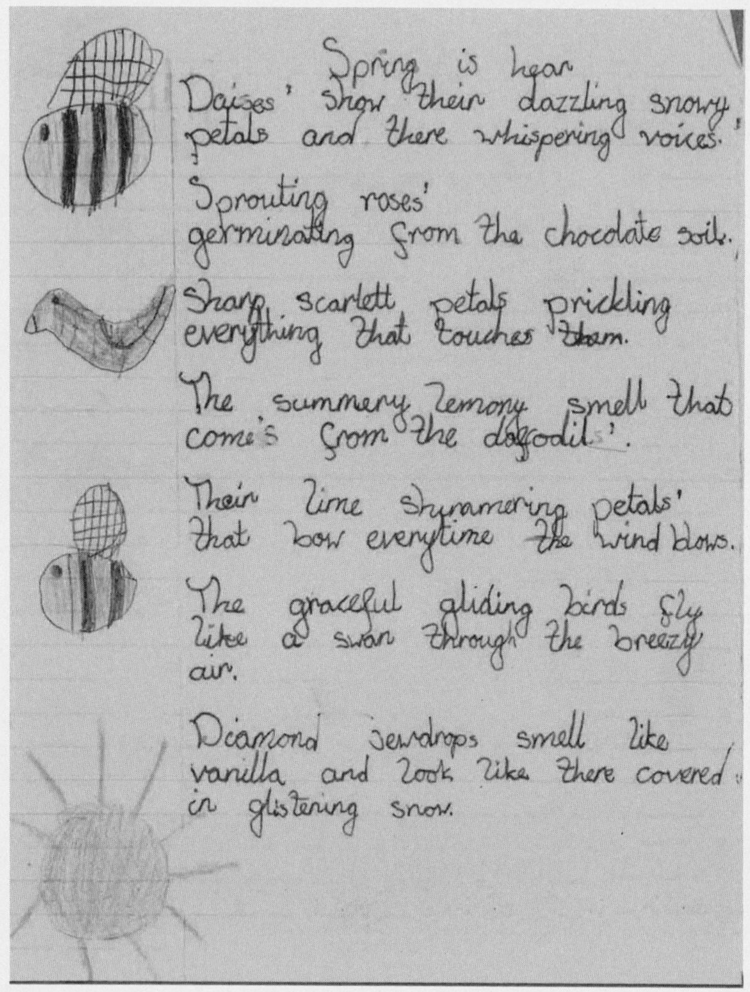

Spring is hear
Daises' show their dazzling snowy
petals and there whispering voices.

Sprouting roses'
germinating from tha chocolate soil.

Sharp scarlett petals prickling
everything that touches them.

The summery lemony smell that
come's from the dafodil's.

Their lime shimmering petals'
that bow everytime the wind blows.

The graceful gliding birds fly
like a swan through the breezy
air.

Diamond jewdrops smell like
vanilla and look like there covered
in glistening snow.

GS

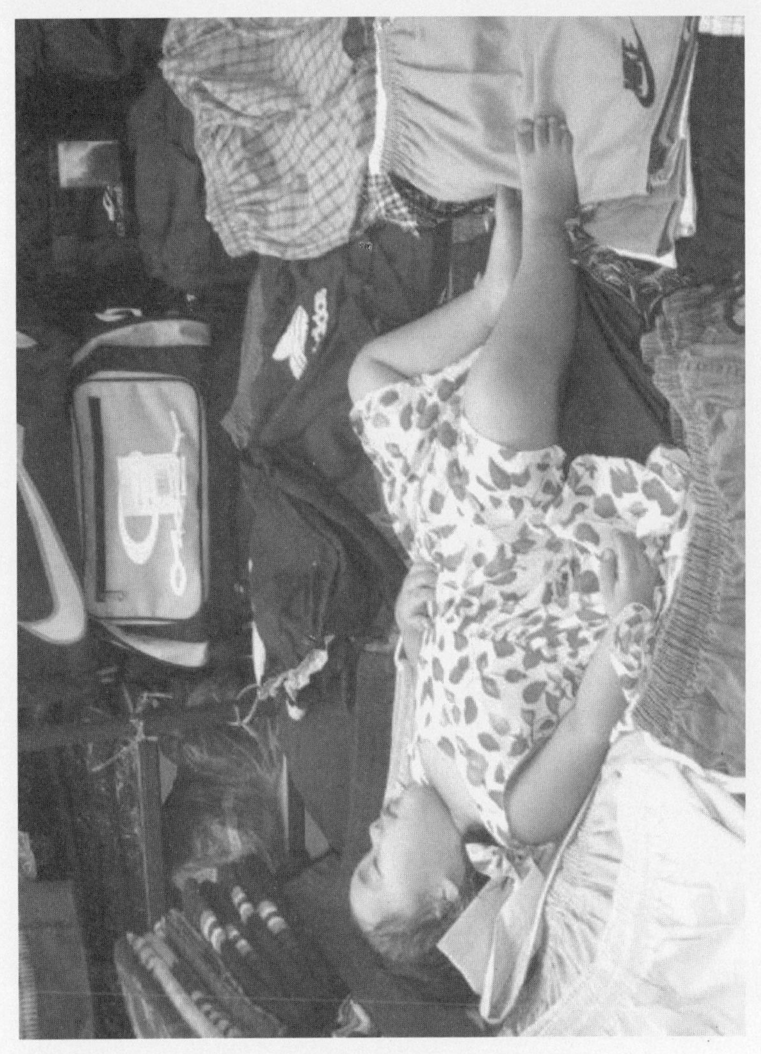

Child for Sale

It
is
more
blessed
to
give
than
to
receive

Holy Bible

*Orandum
est
ut
sit
mens
Sana
In
Corpore
Sano*

Juvenalis

Q. I would like to ask you your opinion on what you think about Rape and about a Rapeline being set up in the UK 24/7?

A. 'I'm appalled at rape, from a male perspective it should never happen even to people who are vulnerable. Any kind of rape is appalling against humanity as a whole.'

A. 'Regarding a rapeline, it is most important because to get help and support is quite difficult for any rape case because most rape cases don't know what to do, who to turn to, they feel embarrassed they don't want to discuss it with family or friends but if they feel there is someone at the end of a phone they can discuss it with its very good.'

Ft. Martin Kershaw (St. Helens)

Light | ◯ Light

JEANETTE SLAVEN, a speech therapist and drama teacher from Cheshire, travelled to the orphanage independently last year. Here she gives her own account of her experience.

"Exactly 12 months ago I boarded a flight to South Africa, heading to Zimbabwe. My mission? To spend time at the Mybua Nehanda orphanage to assist in making a BBC video and to help the innocent victims of Aids, also known locally as Slim. Harare is the world's capital of the disease. A child's life here is over before it's even begun. Children here will sell their body for the price of a loaf of bread.

"A clinic at the centre was very much in demand as gaping wounds, swollen limbs and many other ailments needed instant treatment. Suffering in silence is commonplace, donated medical supplies are always outdated. Yet despite the hardship the children are grateful for a roof over their heads and food in their bellies.

"Conditions were compared by another volunteer to a 'Tenko prison camp'. Latrines are shared and cleaned by the kids, usually the youngest. The stench is unbearable and cleaning substances did not exist. Food is eaten in a huge hall and Sadza, a bland maize porridge, is the staple diet.

"Many of the kids had been molested, abused, abandoned, orphaned. Each individual had their own appalling, sad story but somehow they have a unique pride, faith and dignity and are only too willing to hide their suffering behind smiles."

Extract from MEN, May 3rd 2000

The Dream

I have a dream
  Today I have a dream
    In spite of all the difficulties
    I say I have a dream.

I have a dream
That one day,
The anointed son
Will be head of state.
The son without parents
The son without gardeners
A daughter without a father
A daughter without a mother
I have a dream
  There will be peacemakers

I was sleeping
  Dreaming the dreams of futures
The future of the children
  Children alive, are living on the streets
They will be the shakers of the world
Music makers
Builders of the world
World leaders and world partakers.

Joram Mutazubi, age 14. Zimbabwe

Butchers and the Carpenters Play
Zimbabwe Mbuya Nehanda Orphanage

Poets

are

the

unacknowledged

legislators

of

the

world

Persy Bysshe Shelley

Prick

What am I

I'm a money eating
   Hope defeating
     Social life slaughterer
      And I'm life demeaning.

        I'm a silver temptress
          Evil princess
            Death's white magic
             Nothing less.

            I'm a vein kisser
              Family dismisser
               Depression provider
                Silver widow spider.

              I'm a torture bringer
               Life unhinger,
                Childhood stealer
                 Coffin Sealer.

                  Stephanie Wharton

I am what I am
om.tat.set

Cause for Thoughts

Walking towards the old church,
leaning stones, crosses and angels dominate the entrance.
Both rich and poor resting together,
but both so easily torn apart.
The history of the village wrapped up in dandelions and daises.
Faded sentiments from centuries past,
neighboured by fresh flowers only days old.
A strange peacefulness pervades the air,
although sorrow is so often a visitor.
I sit for a while, untouched.
My mind begins to wander,
then something catches my eye -
the dates 1950-1953.

Christina. E. Romero. Vacas

Sacred Art Restoration

Mystical notes personifying
   Primordial times.
      Flamenco naked notes carrying
       A spine tingling style
        O, to be a muse of this
         Rhythmic fiesta
         As reverend as an
          Aristocratic cante Jondo & Soleà.
        I heard you play bulerías in
       Santa Monica
      A Sacred Art Restoration
     You touched my passion
Duende.

              JS

Revolting

Rectum

Ruthless

Rigid

Rancid

Ravage

Reverberates

Getting Better

Every day in every way,
I'm getting better and better, at . . .

> . . . making coffee
> . . . going to work
> . . . teaching the kids
> . . . watching the birds
> . . . screwing up
> . . . speaking with my mouth full
> . . . forgetting to clean my shoes
> . . . shouting at the neighbours
> . . . getting on with the boss
> . . . making someone else pay for lunch
> . . . being sick all over my friend
> . . . having fun at her expense
> . . . becoming a couch potato
> . . . watching her wash my car
> . . . going out with the pals
> . . . not doing any house work
> . . . having a great row
> . . . winning all the battles

. . . but most of all, keeping the love we have after all these years.

TL

Apt
Myrrh
Guts,Sex
Chocolatte
Orgasm, Foe
Oak'd, Shalom
Mystique, Aqua
Stop,Hysterectomy
Glorification, Divine
Fathomable, Palomino
Exquisite, Principalities
Toxic, Rainbow, Lysitrata
Champagne, Douche, Bare
Embryonic, Zloty, Knowledge
Fantastigorical, Bohemian, Kiss
Omega, Penetration, Affirmative
Atom, Freedom, Retribution, Myth
Serendipity, Dominions, Ginger, Pots
Nectarine, Tarantella, Womb, Bubbles
Homage, Thorn, Eloquence, Freak, Cross
Cornucopia, Cheshirite, Sugary, Vigilante
Universal, Agony, Diva, Barrister, Nightingale
Sensuality, Melodious, Suckets, Antiquity, Alpha
Emerald, Ecstasy, Mirage, Pourri, Bread, Excalibur
Pukka, Lewd, Panacea, Venus, Serpent, Architect, Evil
Phallic , Chalice, Jigsaw, Cocaine, Grape, Barren, Gender
Viagra, Birthday, Virgin, Saviour, Tranquil, Candied, Factor
Crystal, Dolly, Bonbon, Tack, Honeyed, Balls, Potsi, Goddess

A frown is a smile turned upside down
So if you must frown –
Please stand on your head.

Jeanne Peach

My Pride and Joy

I made my babe a bonnet and trimmed it round in blue
with ribbon soft I tied it no greater love I knew
He was my pride and joy

    I made my tot a beret with pom-pom big and bright
    Then popped it on his lovely head and held him to me tight
    He was my pride and joy

I bought my lad a school cap which fell around his ears
I waved him off with heavy heart then shed a mother's tears
He was my pride and joy

    I bought my boy a cub cap he placed it on with pride
    Away he went excitedly and yet again I cried
    He was my pride and joy

I bought my son a scout hat so slim and tall was he
Adventure called and drew him on fearless, strong and free
He was my pride and joy

    I bought my son a baseball cap and marvelled at his skill
    How could my champion ever know my heart was heavy still?
    He was my pride and joy

Who made his balaclava with too slits for his eyes
Who placed the gun into his hand as though he'd won a prize?
Who stole my precious baby my darling baby boy
And made a soldier of the one who was my pride and joy.

Elizabeth Barnard

Heine's Marriage

In 1841 Heine married his mistress, Eugenie Mirat, an assistant in a Paris shoe- shop. This liaison puzzled many of Heine's friends, as Eugenie was vein and silly as well as being totally uneducated. Although the poet sacrificed his social and financial position to marry Eugenie, he was by no means blind to her faults.
when he died he left her all his worldly goods on the condition that she re- married. That way, he said, at least one man would regret his death.

Henrich Heine

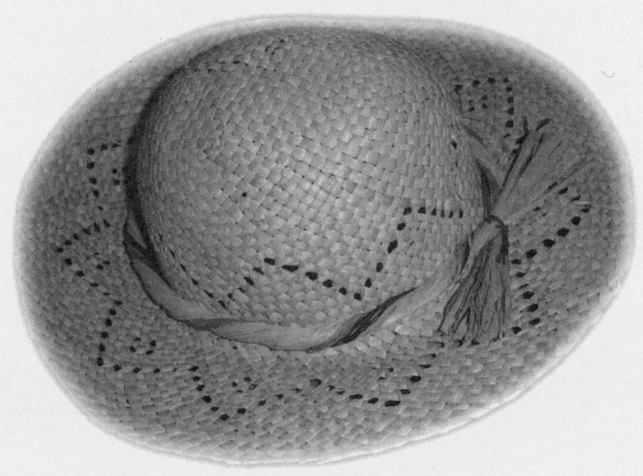

Q. What's your views on Rape and Rapelines?

A. 'Its bad and its taking advantage of someone. Usually someone they know has raped them. Sometimes people are raped and don't really know until the next day, date rape. Teach people when they're younger that helplines are available to them, helplines need more coverage.'

Maureen (Canada)

Q. Could you give me your opinion on Rape please?

A. 'I find it abhorrent I was recently feeling that it was quite upsetting to think that rape is something exclusively committed by men against women.'

Saul Reid (Manchester)

Time

Another year has ended
It is now part of history
A new year is about to blossom
A gift of time - A mystery.

    The old year has gone forever
    With its joy, its pain or sadness
    The future is unknown to us
    The present should fill us with gladness.

The present - the now - is important
Each second of it counts
Time should be spent wisely
It gains interest in God's account.

    Time is a gift from God
    More precious than silver or gold
    Time is on loan to you and me
    It cannot be bought or sold.

Never waste this precious commodity
By needless worry or anxiety
Ignore the forecasters of gloom
Present in our society.

    Be alert to see another's need
    Forgive those who offend us
    Be charitable in words and deed
    The Good Lord will commend us.

Sometimes darkness shrouds our pathway
We give in to despair
Have faith Our Friend has planned the way
And he is always there.

God can be seen and heard
In every human creature
we are made in his image and likeness
He is our greatest teacher.

Let us be diligent at our work
And enjoy our recreations
Take time to pray, reflect on each day
Thank God for blessings, for consolations.

Let love O Lord be the motive
Of everything we do
Whether our efforts be large or small
We offer them back to you.

So as we embark on a new year
Trust in Our lord's protection
The present, the future, the unknown
Are under His direction.

Time is a valuable treasure
Do not be troubled by fears
have faith, have courage, and hope in God
And leave to Him - The Years.

Monica Doherty

Urbanite

Smile

Take this smile I give you wherever you may go . . .
And when you see another smile you will surely know
that I am always with you in everything you see . . .
A crowded train, a soaring plane, a ship upon the sea.
And every face that smiles at you will probably be me.

No matter where you wander throughout the coming years,
I will wish just smiles for you and never any tears.
And should you ever need me, you know where I will be,
searching every passing face for your sweet smile to see.!

Peasants & Paupers Poetry Circle

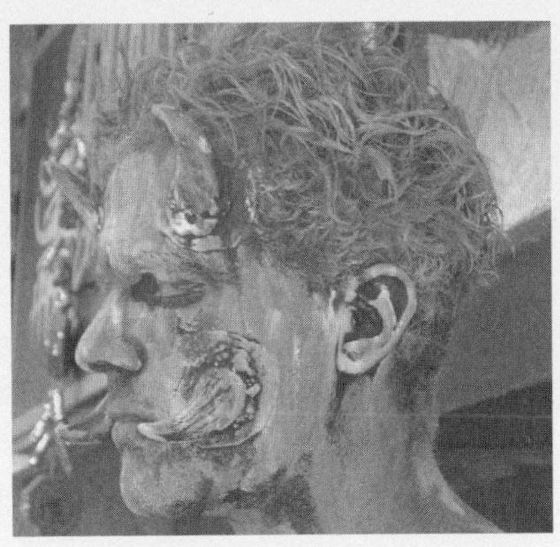

Compassion

We're animal lovers in Britain they say
But I find it hard to believe,
When beautiful birds are shot from the sky
And all I can do is grieve.

Live cows, pigs and sheep are transported abroad
Along endless roads and o'er water,
To arrive on the continent broken and scared
And then cruelly taken for slaughter.

Hens kept in cages so small they can't move
No sunshine and no sky of blue
They're 'egg-machines' - can't we do something for them?
Would you like to live as they do?

There's hunting with dogs - I despair when I think
Of the fox and the hare and the deer
Being hounded for hours, they have no chance at all,
It's heart breaking to think of their fear.

Animals used for testing cosmetics,
Fur farming for somebody's fashion,
Ostriches, Kangaroo's, Beagle's who smoke,
What's happened to love and compassion?

We're all living beings, we all feel the pain
Creatures, including us, need sunshine and rain.
There must be a better way these tortures must cease,
respect these poor animals and leave them in peace.

Margaret Doherty

5 Legged Jesus

Whilst studying a pastel 'crowd scene' of Lowry's in my friend
Selwyn Demmy's art collection my roving eye discovered a five
legged mongrel! The creature lay upon its back, stiffened limbs
reaching for the sky with a cat on either side, Lowry sketched at
Mid Day studios in Manchester where two stray moggies
Modigliani and Hobbema kept the mice away, perhaps in this
picture the mutt was their prey.
 Further research revealed the artist friend, Dr. Laing (atheist &
eccentric) was master of a five legged dog named 'Jesus.' Dr. Laing
would often take his pet on hospital visits, much to the amusement
of Ashton Infirmary.

JS

HE WHO KNOWS HIMSELF,

KNOWS EVERYONE.

HE WHO CAN LOVE HIMSELF,

LOVES EVERYONE

ST AUGUSTUS OF EYGPT

BE A SAINT WHILST STILL HERE AND NOW

Secrets of a Rape Victim

Messed up, sadness and despair
Guilt complex. You are not there
In my life of caring for.
I miss you so much, each day more
What should I do? My life is Hell.
Time passes by, then all goes well
Until the phone rings and I hear my name.
There is my son, tears, emotion and shame.
I begin to panic, have doubts in my heart
Does it make sense? It tears me apart!
Mountains of sorrow are rising up
All the secrets inside, can they finally stop?
Be proud and start to explain..................?
Doing that, will there be any less pain?
Having been raped will never heal.
I have a son and only I know what I feel.

                              Anonymous

Something that is stronger
And deeper than any words
Is found in love.

                              Author Unknown

Words are of course a very powerful drug.

*Ninety per cent of the Friction of daily
    life is caused by Tone of Voice*

*Speak only with your Heart and your
    Soul.*

Jeanne Peach

Water Exit

As we stand high above the ocean
Two feet from the edge
One thousand'th from the ocean,
A storm is blowing
An acceleration of lightening
Wild winds, salt water moistens the air
Water explodes against the rocks
Your hand trembles, my eardrums roar
Like thunder sledded from
Rock to rock
Water flooding my mind as it
Flogs at the cliff.
Our hearts on fire we stare, lips touch
We have no more hand to grip
Walk two feet we slip easily
Like pebbles from a split sack.
Water we are no more.

Anthony Fahye

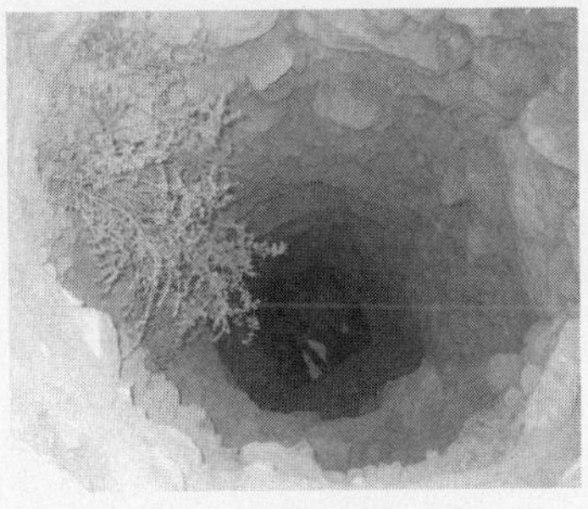

Water Well

The Fat Fairy

Down in the garden where no body goes
   Lives a fat fairy who does not wear clothes
      She tried all the shops to find something to fit
         But as hard as she tries she gets stuck with the zip.

      Every evening she sits under a stone
      and wishes she wasn't always alone
   Then one night a glow worm walks by
He has a light on his tail and a gleam in his eye

Follow me fat fairy and don't be so glum
   I'll find you something to fit over your tum
      My friend is a tailor and spins a fine web
         he works in the corner at the back of the shed

   He will make you a dress that is measured to fit
And don't be afraid there wont be a zip

The tailor he spun the whole night through
   He created a dress and a pretty hat too
      The fairy she danced and sung with such glee
         She knocked all the nuts off the hazelnut tree

      So no longer does the fat fairy sit all alone
      The glow worm loves her and they have set up a home
   They sit in the garden during the day
And if you are quite you can hear them at play.

                                        G. Fernley

pax

Give Me Your Vote!

Give me your vote, the candidate wrote, from the local political
party....
And if I'm elected, I'll do what's expected and roll up my sleeves and
get
started. I'll do this and that, 'Yakerty yak, yakerty, yakerty,
yarty'....
I won't let you down, if you come around and give your vote to our
party.

Give me your vote, the candidate wrote, and to be perfectly
honest dear madam,
I'm really sincere, and understanding your fears.. Although I
don't know you from' Adam!
'Yakerty yak, yakerty yakerty, yarty'. Just slip on your coat,
come along and vote, for our caring political party!

Give me your vote, the candidate wrote, from the local political
party...
And I'll cut waiting list for the cures of cyst, lumbago, piles and
arteries...
aching backs, heart attacks, rickets and rampant arthritis.
'Yakerty yak, yakerty
yakerty, yarty'. Don't give up hope, give us your vote, a vote for the
health
caring party.

So I gave my vote to the candidate who wrote, from the local
political party...
who seemed really honest, with no cause to admonish, but alas
and alack...
he never wrote back, with his' Yakerty yak, yakerty, yakerty,
yarty,!'....
He no longer needs me, since the victory of his caring political
party.

The moral is thus, don't ever trust Any political party, who promise
you 'this..
and promise you 'that' with their 'Yakerty yak, yakerty, yakerty,
yarty,' when
all they are doing is cunningly 'wooing' and doing their best to
feather the nest...
for themselves and the rest ... of their 'caring' political party!

                                        Peasants & Paupers Poetry Circle

Payment

2

Day?

My Day

I've had a pig of a day.
The boss put obstacles in my way.
That's bosses for you.

    My daughter and I had a row
    She thinks I'm a silly old cow.
    That's teenagers for you.

I was busy as a bee
Cooking something special for tea,
But did he notice? No, not he.
That's husbands for you.

    I worked like a dog
    For a boss no better than a hog,
    And a husband as blind as a bat.

So I'm sick as a parrot tonight.
I nearly won the lottery, but not quite.
That tenner would have come in handy.

    Any why, you ask, did I never let slip the mask,
    But stayed quiet as the quietest church mouse?
    Well, I guess I'm just a chicken.

Now I really must fly,
Bedtime draws nigh,
And one thing remains to be done.

    Just for a hoot,
    I'll get drunk as a newt,
    And hope that tomorrow's more fun.

Sue Mather

Cobbler, Cobbler Mend My Shoe

Friendship

Real friends are hard to find
But without you I'd be blind!
our friendship will always show
The whole world is going to know
That you and I are two of a kind.
Together forever in heart and mind!
We'll stay together until the end
You and I are the best of friends.

Catherine Hardman

Sunny Survivor

Saddest of all is the aftermath.

Sunny child, outgoing and strong,
Now sullen, withdrawn and weak.
A spark. A spitfire. A ball of sudden fury.

I wanted to tell Dad
But, when the chance came,
I couldn't speak.

Don't !'
The word spat itself out
Before I could put a guard on my lip.
don't touch.
Don't discuss.
Don't kiss.'
'Why?'
'Just don't'

Frozen in time. Icy embryo of potential love;
Of potential giving.
Freezing cold; guarding; watching; wary.
No one could reach me. No one could comfort me.

In a cocoon of silence
That I weave about myself
I heal myself - and learn to love and trust.
Painfully. Slowly. It takes years.

So loving and warm now;
So cold and rejecting then.
Sunny. Happy. Accepting.

What secret lives people live.

Jean-Noelle Aires

great nana age
<u>93</u>
Loves
Robbie Williams
Adam 10 years

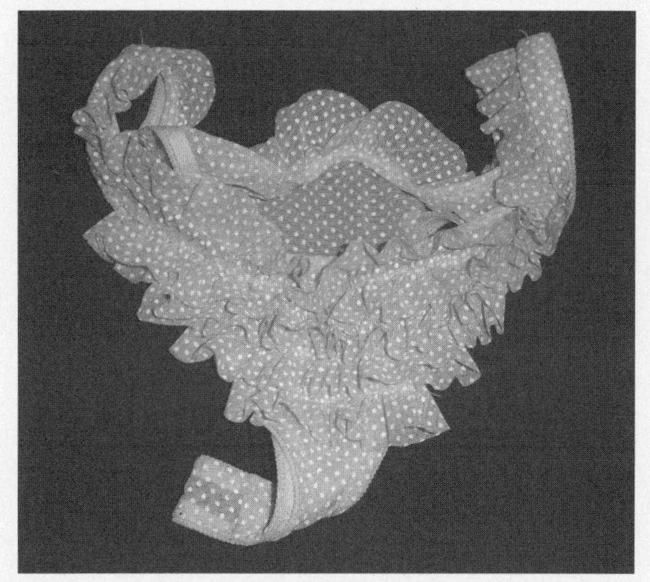

Lou-Lou's Nik-Niks

What is 'Linedance' in Spanish ???

'Is this Casa Cultura?'
I asked the man outside
'No, Senorita ..... I dunno'
(We really need a guide)

    'I'll explain, por favor, senior
    I want to Linedance please ....
    I have my dance shoes in my bag
    So put my mind at ease ....

I haven't danced since we arrived
And it's my greatest wish
To Linedance in Majorca
Come with us - if you wish....

    My husband's getting anxious
    He knows I need a 'fix'
    Then he can pop off to the bar
    And have a cocktail mix.....

The man outside just looked at me
A smile came to his face
'No comprendo Linedance'
This place - The Donkey Race!!!!!

Margaret Doherty

REMEMBER LOVE

No More Place to

Go.
No control over my body
No power upon my soul...

    Lost here I am again
    Nowhere to go
    Nothing left at all...

        But as time goes by
        So as my pain
        So as my hope...
        Its time to get up
        Its time to set myself free
        Time to rise...

Start all over again
Turn my lights on
Change the old song...

        Get over the past
        Forget the tale
        Leave the tears.

    So...I say...
    Let's move on
    And let the past go.

        No more pain
        No more sorrow
        No more yesterday

        So...I say
        Let's start again
        And beat up the past...

Roger Rezende

Dream Recipe

A heart full of love
  Angel xxxx's
    Beams of Sunshine
      Moon Light Wishes
        Silvery Stars & Rainbows
          Crystallised Snowflakes
            Pure white Down & Roses
              Crumbly Layer Cake
                Fragrant Jasmine Petals
                  Raindrops Heaven sent
                    Oyster Pearls & World Peace
                      Dreamiest Dreams ever Dreamt.

                Mix & Spice with inspirational imagination
                Sleep until its done!!!

                                        JS

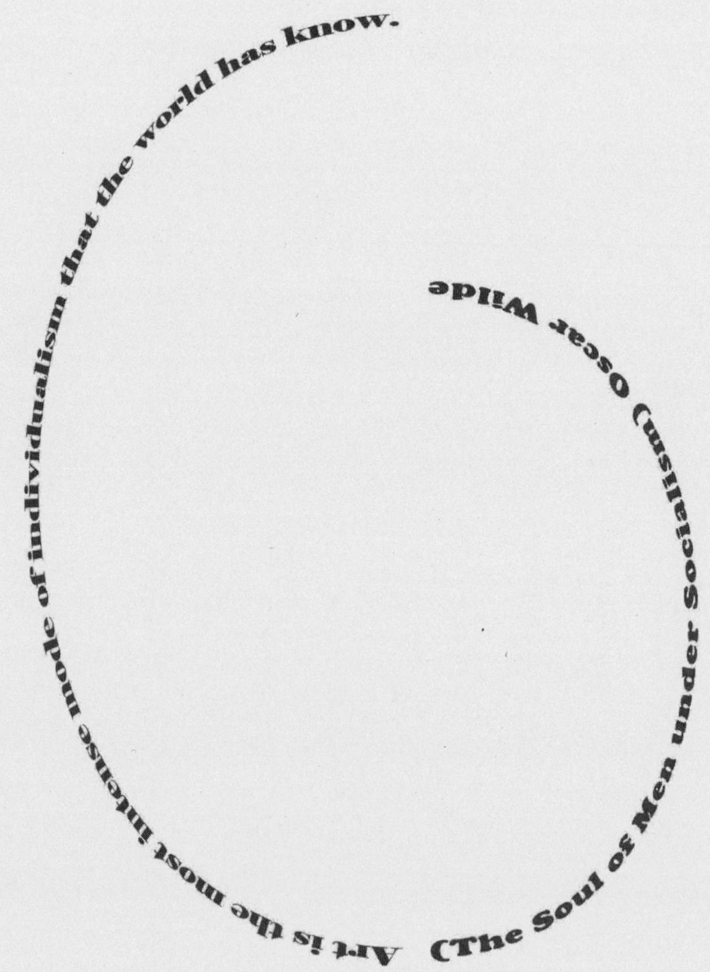

Art is the most intense mode of individualism that the world has know.
(The Soul of Men under Socialism) Oscar Wilde

♥eArt

OnLy 1

fOr

U

Cosmopolitan Coktale

Cosmopolitan World
Cosmopolitan Girl
Cosmopolitan Boy
Cosmopolitan Love
Cosmopolitan Child
Cosmopolitan Race
Cosmopolitan Laws
Cosmopolitan Rules
Cosmopolitan Rhetoric
Cosmopolitan Confusion
Cosmopolitan Power
Cosmopolitan War
Cosmopolitan Greed
Cosmopolitanly Cosmopolitan
Cosmopolitan Homily
Cosmopolitan Grace
Cosmopolitan Belief
Cosmopolitan Faith
Cosmopolitan Cuisine
Cosmopolitanly Served
Cosmopolitan Coktale?

Shaken not stirred.!!

JS

Justice